WHISPERS TO YOGANANDA

RENU SINGH PARMAR

ISBN 979-888546633-2

These 'whispers' are dedicated to **Sri Sri Paramhansa Yogananda**, my beloved Guru in this life and in the lives to come...

Sri Sri Paramhansa Yogananda(5.1.1893-7.3.1952)

Contents

Preface   *vii*

Prologue   *ix*

1. All I Know   1

2. Thy Grace   3

3. I Need Your Help   5

4. Keep Me Close   7

5. Master Peace   9

6. Maya   11

7. Your Will   13

8. Divine Sculptor   15

9. Let Me Not Forget   17

10. I Cling To You   19

11. To You   21

12. The Light   23

13. When The Tears Flow   25

14. Your Stubborn Child   26

15. The Razor's Edge   28

16. You Are On My Side   30

17. Make Me Humble   32

Preface

On 26th January 2002, at the Yogoda Satsanga Society(YSS) ashram at Dakshineshwar, Kolkatta, I took my first set of YSS lessons on self-realization, written my Guru, Sri Sri Paramhansa Yoganandaji. Since then, I have tried to follow my beloved Gurudev's teachings as far as I sincerely can. Guruji has rightly said, "The path to God is like a razor's edge. But discouragement is never justified because we don't have to acquire or win anything; we have only to realize that God is within us." Walking on the razor's edge is not easy at all but with His Grace and blessings, one can, despite the cuts and falls.

Learning to love oneself, in spite of one's flaws and failures, is an important lesson I have learnt from Him. Despite best efforts, one may fail and fail again on the Path of righteousness, but that should not discourage us from trying again and again, because He is always there guiding us, lovingly showing us the way. He has given us great hope when he says, "If you think I am near, I am near." And indeed He is! I realize that my life would have been entirely different had I not been blessed and accepted by my Guru. All I can say is that I cannot live without His love and guidance. I tell Him, even as Divine Mother told Him: "Always have I loved Thee, ever will I love Thee!"

This collection of 'whispers', are the outpourings of my heart to my divine Guru, on His 129th birth anniversary, 5th January 2022. It also marks two decades of my discipleship at His lotus feet.

Prologue

Sri Sri Paramhansa Yogananda

Paramhansa Yogananda, or Mukund Lal Ghosh, was born on 5th January 1893 in Gorakhpur, U.P. to pious Bengali parents, who were ardent devotees of Sri Sri Lahiri Mahasaya of Benaras.

When baby Mukund was in his mother's arms, Lahiri Mahasaya blessed Him and addressed His mother, "Little mother, thy son will be a Yogi. As a spiritual engine, He will carry many souls to God's kingdom." Lahiri Mahasaya Himself had been blessed by the deathless Mahavatar Babaji with the technique of Kriya which had been lost to man over the centuries.

It was in 1910, when Mukund was 17, that He met His Guru, Sri Sri Yukteshwarji in Benaras. For the next 10 years, He was blessed with spiritual guidance from his Guru in the latter's ashrams in Srirampur and Puri. Swami Yukteshwarji revealed to Yogananda the plan of Mahavatar Babaji to send Him to America to spread the ancient science of Kriya there and worldwide.

In 1915, Mukund took His final vows as a monk and was bestowed the name of Yogananda, signifying bliss through Divine Union, by His Guru, Swami Yukteshwarji.

In 1917, he founded a 'how to live' school for boys and the Yogoda Satsanga Society(YSS) in Ranchi. It was in 1920 that He had a vision of going to America to fulfil Mahavatar Babaji's mission and arrived in Boston to deliver a lecture on the 'Science of Religion' at the International Congress of Religious Liberals. It was in the same year that he founded the Self Realization Fellowship(SRF) in Boston and later the international headquarters at Mt. Washington, Los Angeles, in 1925.

From 1924 to 1935, Swamiji travelled and lectured widely and was very well received by the American public at large. He emphasized the underlying unity of the world's greatest religions and taught universally applicable methods for attaining the direct personal experience of God through meditation and scientific techniques.

In 1935 he made a final visit to India to meet His Guru who bestowed on Him the highest spiritual title of 'Paramhansa'(supreme swan).

It was in the 1930s that He began putting together the guidance and instructions He had given to students as YSS lessons for home study. He also devoted Himself to writing '**Autobiography of a Yogi'**, the spiritual classic that has now been translated into over 50 languages. Apart from this book, His most seminal and voluminous works are His interpretations of the Bhagwad Gita and the Bible i.e. **God Talks With Arjuna** and the **Second Coming of Christ**, respectively.

On March 7 1952, the great Guru entered Mahasamadhi, the conscious exit from the body by a God realized soul. His last words were a poem on His beloved India.

Paramhansa Yogananda , the highly revered world teacher and Guru to millions around the world, was one of the greatest emissaries to the west of India's ancient wisdom mainly the paths of meditation and kriya yoga. His life and teachings are a source of light and inspiration to people of all races, cultures and creeds.

Jai Guru !

1. All I Know

All I know is that
I will love You always
As You have loved me
Through the ages.
All I know is that
I shall follow You
No matter how steep the climb,
How dangerous the places
That I reach,
As I defy You in my waywardness.
All I know is that
You will be there
To welcome me back,
The prodigal child,
Who wandered off,
But knowing that home
Was only one place:
In Your arms.
All I know is that
I am ultimately
One with You,
We are One.

2. Thy Grace

Suddenly with Thy Grace,
it has become easier to let go
of all the distractions
all the temptations
that kept me bound
to my mortal being.
Bless me on this journey
Of realization,
And free me from the coils of delusion
That has kept me entrapped,
Like a bird in a cage,
Wanting to fly,
But pinned down
By desires.
You have opened up the skies for me
Letting me see the vast vistas
That can be mine…
Let me not falter now,
Lovingly, nudge me onwards
Into the Light
That is rightfully mine.
Help me to walk on the thorns

As if non existed.
I have bled many times on them.
But now the gravel and the rock
Are less treacherous.
I can cross the chasm
With Thy loving care.

3. I Need Your Help

Your Path is not a bed of roses.
It is scattered with jagged stones and thorns
That I must walk on …or avoid…
According to my will…
And when I do,
I must not complain about how I bleed.
The options You give me
Are very clear…
Either steer clear or get hurt.
Even when I say:
"According to Thy will",
I carelessly meander into
Treacherous territory,
Letting my mortal body and mind
Take the cut and thrust
Of blinding delusion.
Your Path shines golden
…way past the
Thorns and stubble…
To get there, I must tread carefully,
Picking myself past
The sudden blinding flashes

Of Maya,
That fell me for a while.
Come, help me
To get beyond Her,
My Guru,
For I am Thy Golden child.

4. Keep Me Close

The clatter of worldly activity
And the noise of careless words,
Lead me into the tiring
Ways of the world
That keeps me enthralled for a while…
But soon enough
I feel tired in my bones,
Mind and soul…
At the resounding hollowness
Of it all.
Please keep me close always,
Even when I step out
From Your loving Presence
Into the din of everyday living.
Peel away the layers of my carelessness,
Of my rebelliousness,
So that I may shine again
With Your love,
So bright and beautiful.
May I not have to ask You
To bring me back,
Let Your Presence always remind me

That You are with me
Forever and forever,
Whether in the task of daily routine,
Or when I meditate on You,
And coax You to my
Altar of love.

5. Master Peace

When the waves of the highs and lows
Have played out
And I am finally on an even keel,
I shall know that You have blessed me
With the touch of Your peace.
When the storms of trials
Feel but a gentle breeze,
I shall know
That I have finally
Boarded Your boat of stillness.
I shall try, I shall try
To sandpaper the jagged peaks
Of happiness
And thrusts of sadness
To bring forth
An even graph
that You will gladly
Put me on,
Even as I face trials
Every other day.

6. Maya

The whiplashes of Maya I submit to
Feel like gentle caresses,
Till I fall headlong into the chasm
Of my desires, my temptations
That never end.
Even as I see Your hand
Outstretched to pull me out,
I hesitate like a frightened bird,
Unsure of my ability
To soar to freedom.
Just keep at me-
Keep telling me
That You are mine
And I am Yours
And that You will never let me
Be taken away by delusion,
that trips me up often,
leads me away to
a mirage of joys
that vanishes as soon as
I get caught in its trap.
Thank You

For coming to drag me out,
now and then,
from the dungeons of my errors,
and to save me from myself.

7. Your Will

Oh, Guru!
I bring trouble upon myself
And then run to You for help
--like a child up to mischief,
Knowing that You will find a way
For Your obstinate child.
But I must do my bit...
I must reason, will and act...
You won't do everything for me.
You are my Will
You are my Reason,
You shall be my Action.
So guide me to see
Your Will,
To see Your Will!

8. Divine Sculptor

This morning hour
So beauteous with Your Presence,
Pulls me into Your arms
Of peace and protection,
I am inundated in the light of Your love.
How can I go wrong…
But, I do…
During the harsh blaze of the day,
I find myself in recalcitrant moods,
Tempestuous sometimes,
Sometimes resentful.
But with Your loving prod,
I come back to equilibrium,
Heeding Your soft whispers,
That guide me back to righteousness
And acceptance…
Surrender I will to You…
For You have taken my sins
And will pave my Path
With all that I need:
The rocks and the pebbles,
The roses and the thorns…

Do with me as You will,
For I know
It is for my own good.
O Divine Sculptor,
Chisel Thou my life
To Thy Design!

9. Let Me Not Forget

You know, I can't live without You,
You are my life,
You are my love …
You are the breath,
You are the Pran,
You are the light in my eyes…
Keep me attuned to You…
Whisper Your messages into my soul.
May I read Your glances right,
May I feel the tendrils of Your love.
What other love do I need
But Yours…
For the glitter of this world
Passes by like a blimp…
Transient, short-lived.
You are my only constant,
My only wish.
Let me not forget You
In the clamour of noisy routine.
For You, will I do all
For You, I will surrender all…
Whether working, sleeping,

Meditating, walking, eating,
Anything…
Everything for You…
My life is for You…
I will not forget,
Let me not forget.

10. I Cling to You

I cling to You,
I am like the baby monkey
Clinging to its mother.
I cling to You,
For life, for breath,
Without You, I cannot live…
Every day I tell You:
Do what You want of me.
In You I trust,
In You I give myself.
I cling to You…
Let Maya not take me away,
I cling to You
Your love is all I need.
I cling to You,
Take me on the journey
That You have planned for me.
I surrender,
I surrender!

11. To You

Lord,

You have made these equations

very simple:

I don't have to go into contortions

of mental enquiry

to find the answers.

You have brought them

right in front of me :

You, You, You,

Every answer is You,

Every wonder is You,

Every happiness is You,

Every sadness is You.

You are the clouds

that drift slowly by

You are the beauteous sunset

that brings me joy.

You are the hot sun,

You are the cool breeze,

You are everything.

Can I ever thank You enough,

O, Guru?

Not for that which You give,
But for the understanding
without which I cannot live.

12. The Light

I still try to grasp the tail
of worldly success
But let it slip away
without much effort.
It does not really matter
any more.
The new world You show me
promises much more…
How can I hanker after tinsel
when Your million suns
are upon me?

13. When The Tears Flow

When the tears flow,
Know that they are for You.
When the tears flow,
Know that I pine for You.
When the tears flow
I know that
You have blessed me.
When the tears flow
I know that
You have baptized me.

14. Your Stubborn Child

Oh, Guru! Why don't You
talk to me anymore?
When earlier Your voice
Would ring out in my dreams,
Or suddenly flash
A message of reassurance….
of guidance.
You have left me
To divine You through
My lowly resources,
Diminished as they are
By the veils of Maya….
Have You given up on me?
The cantankerous, stubborn child
Who persists in her
inconsistent ways,
Yet grasps Your robe
in desperation.
But I need You, I do, I do…
Without Your whispers,
How can I survive
On my erroneous interpretations,

On my ego-guided reasoning?
Tear away the purdah of delusion,
Tell me, even if I'm not worthy,
That You will speak to me,
Hold me, lead me,
Out of this darkness of doubt,
And wavering faith.
For I want to hear
Your voice, loud and clear
Or as a melodious whisper.
I must, I must,
I insist, I insist
Like Your tantrum-prone child…
Will You not give in?

15. The Razor's Edge

The razor's edge
is what I walk on,
As You have ordained, dear Guru.
I cut and bleed every day,
trying not to do what
my mortal self tells me…
Everyday You send
the whispers of Maya
to sing tunes of temptation
into my mind,
which listens
till
the soul call brings me back
inline,
when I find
You have put me back
on the razor
that shall cut me once again,
maybe not so deeply,
but bleed again I must.
I know by now
That defeat and victory

are both transient,
Like the days and nights,
Till You decide
I have had enough
Of the ups and downs,
and embrace me
into Your very Own-ness.
I shall wait, Guru......
After all,
You have chosen me.

16. You Are On My Side

Some things happen
to take me away
from Your Path.
My mortal self hopes to finish off
these distractions in this birth,
So that in the next
they do not reappear.
....or will they ? .....
I look at this arrival
From my past life :
It wasn't finished then.....
and now comes back full circle......
Maybe it has yet
to be written off by Karma,
it has yet to be drained
from the river in my spine
into the vast ocean of Spirit,
Before I can claim
Certainty in Eternity.
Will you forgive me, my Guru?
for this regression......
I will carry the cross

that must weigh me down
in this life.
But I will resurrect, as I must
For You are on my side .....

17. Make Me Humble

*Make me humble
Oh, Gurudev,
so that I may receive
Your benediction
and guidance.*

*Bestow on me
the quietness of heart
of the little one in the corner.
Take from me the I, Me, Mine,
that I may behold
the grossness of this body,
of this world.*

*Take from me
my desires of mortal greatness
for they are but
flimsy trappings
spun by the spider of delusion.*

*Take me away
from the tumults of the heart*

that grieves for gone byes
and keeps me swamped
in the past.

May I see only today
as it unfolds
beauteously before me,
unburdened by past follies
and future aspirations.

Take away the hydra-headed
Maya of earthly demands
and refurbish me simple and sweet,
full of the frankincense
of Your Presence.

Make me Your innocent child,
guileless, happy, trusting...
Make me like Yourself
Oh, Gurdev!